Up Words for Down Days

Up Words for Down Days

Compiled by Allen Klein

Gramercy Books
New York

This 1998 edition is published by Gramercy Books, an imprint of Random House Value
Publishing, a division of Random House, Inc., New York.

Gramercy is a registered trademark and the colophon is a trademark of Random House, Inc.

Random House
New York • Toronto • London • Sydney • Auckland
www.randomhouse.com

Editor: Donna Lee Lurker
Designer: Debra Borg

Printed and bound in the United States of America

Library of Congress Cataloging-in-Publication Data
Up words for down days / complied by Allen Klein
p.   cm.
Includes index.
ISBN 0-517-20270-0
1. Quotations. 2 Wit and humor. I. Klein, Allen.
PN6084.H8U62   1998
082—dc21   98-27016
CIP

8 7

For my mom,
who has often had an
up word for my down day

CONTENTS

INTRODUCTION

The quotations in this book are sometimes wise, sometimes witty. But they are always helpful.

When they are wise, they can lend a hand in helping you overcome your tough times. And when they are witty, they will give you a different view of your solemn situation—and nothing, perhaps, gives a better perspective than a good laugh.

In either case, pick this book up when you, or someone you know, needs a lift. One reader of my previous quote book, *Quotations to Cheer You Up When the World Is Getting You Down*, told me that each day she E-mailed a quote from that book to her ailing mother. She said that not only did it cheer her mother up, but selecting the quotes helped the reader too.

While the quotes in that book were designed around positive words, like "happy," "joy," "laughter," etc., those in this book focus on trying times, such as "aging," "diet and exercise," "stress and burnout," etc. As in *Quotations to Cheer You Up*, these quotes can be used in a variety of ways:

- Pick up the book, randomly open to a quote, and let those words be your guiding thought for the day or the week.

- Use these quotes as you would any reference book—in speeches, on bulletin boards, in newsletters, etc.

- Read a section at a time and savor its wisdom and wit.

However you use them, my hope is that the uplifting quotations in this book will provide a lesson or a laugh to help you get through your down days.

Allen Klein, San Francisco
www.allenklein.com

A quotation
at the right moment
is like bread
in a famine.
The Talmud

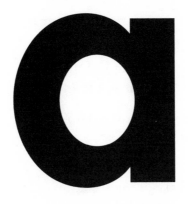

age & aging
anger & adversity

age *n* the length of time that one has existed

ag•ing *v* the process of growing old or maturing

Age is a question of mind over matter.
If you don't mind, it doesn't matter.
Satchel Paige

I was born in 1962. True.
And the room next to me was 1963.
Joan Rivers

I'm not interested in age.
People who tell their age are silly.
You're as old as you feel.
Elizabeth Arden

Age is not important
unless you're a cheese.
Helen Hayes

The prime of life is that fleeting time
between green and over-ripe.
Cullen Hightower

My mother always used to say:
"The older you get, the better you get,
unless you're a banana."
Rose Nylund in The Golden Girls

Wisdom doesn't automatically come with old age.
Nothing does—except wrinkles.
It's true, some wines improve with age.
But only if the grapes were good in the first place.
Abigail Van Buren

Old age isn't so bad when you consider the alternative.
Maurice Chevalier

The secret of staying young is to live honestly,
eat slowly, and lie about your age.
Lucille Ball

It's paradoxical that the idea of living a long life
appeals to everyone, but the idea of getting old
doesn't appeal to anyone.
Andy Rooney

Thirty-five is a very attractive age.
London society is full of women of the highest birth
who have, of their own free choice,
remained thirty-five for years.
Oscar Wilde

Life begins at forty.
Walter B. Pitkin

To be seventy years young is sometimes far more cheerful
and hopeful than to be forty years old.
Oliver Wendell Holmes

I've always roared with laughter when they say life begins at forty.
That's the funniest remark ever. The day I was born
was when life began for me.
Bette Davis

A woman past forty should make up her mind
to be young—not her face.
Billie Burke

Now that I'm over sixty I'm veering toward respectability.
Shelley Winters

I'm over the hill, but the climb was terrific!
Graffiti

Just remember, once you're over the hill,
you begin to pick up speed.
Charles Schulz

Old age is like a plane flying through a storm.
Once you're aboard, there's nothing you can do.
Golda Meir

The trick is growing up without growing old.
Casey Stengel

You can't help getting older,
but you don't have to get old.
George Burns

If you carry your childhood with you,
you never become older.
Abraham Sutzkever

Whatever a man's age may be,
he can reduce it several years by putting
a bright-colored flower in his buttonhole.
Mark Twain

When it comes to staying young,
a mind-lift beats a face-lift any day.
Marty Bucella

Everyone is the age of their heart.
Guatemalan saying

We are always the same age inside.
Gertrude Stein

I'll tell ya how to stay young:
Hang around with older people.
Bob Hope

Being middle-aged is a nice change from being young.
Dorothy Canfield Fisher

Middle age is when you've met so many people
that every new person you meet
reminds you of someone else.
Ogden Nash

Middle age is when your age starts to show
around your middle.
Bob Hope

Don't worry about middle age:
you'll outgrow it.
Laurence J. Peter

You know you are getting old when people tell you
how good you look.
Alan King

You know you are getting old when the candles
cost more than the cake.
Bob Hope

I smoke cigars because at my age
if I don't have something to hang onto I might fall down.
George Burns

I have everything now that I had twenty years ago—
except now it's all lower.
Gypsy Rose Lee

They tell you that you'll lose your mind when you grow
older. What they don't tell you
is that you won't miss it very much.
Malcolm Cowley

There are three signs of old age. Loss of memory...
I forget the other two.
Red Skelton

My grandfather's a little forgetful, but he likes to give me advice.
One day, he took me aside and left me there.
Ron Richards

First you forget names, then you forget faces,
then you forget to pull your zipper up,
then you forget to pull your zipper down.
Leo Rosenberg

My dad's pants kept creeping up on him.
By sixty-five he was just a pair of pants and a head.
Jeff Altman

One of the many pleasures of old age is giving things up.
Malcolm Muggeridge

I look forward to being older,
when what you look like becomes less and less an issue
and what you are is the point.
Susan Sarandon

There is many a good tune played on an old fiddle.
Old saying

There is a fountain of youth; it is your mind, your talents, the creativity
you bring to your life and the lives of the people you love. When you
will learn to tap this source, you will have truly defeated age.
Sophia Loren

I never feel age....
If you have creative work,
you don't have age or time.
Louise Nevelson

I want to tell people approaching and perhaps fearing age that it is a
time of discovery. If they say "Of what?"
I can only answer "We must find out for ourselves,
otherwise it won't be discovery."
Florida Scott-Maxwell

Anyone can get old.
All you have to do is live long enough.
Groucho Marx

How old would you be
if you didn't know how old you are?
Satchell Paige

Don't complain about growing old—
many people don't have that privilege.
Earl Warren

an•ger *n* a strong feeling of hostility or displeasure

ad•ver•si•ty *n* a state of hardship or distress

This makes me so sore it gets my dandruff up.
Samuel Goldwyn

The best remedy for a short temper is a long walk.
Jacqueline Schiff

Anyone can become angry. That is easy.
But to be angry with the right person, to the right degree,
at the right time, for the right purpose
and in the right way—that is not easy.
Aristotle

As a girl my temper often got out of bounds.
But one day when I became angry at a friend
over some trivial matter, my mother said to me,
"Elizabeth, anyone who angers you conquers you."
Sister Elizabeth Kenny

The greatest remedy for anger is delay.
Seneca

Grow angry slowly—there's plenty of time.
Ralph Waldo Emerson

Speak when you are angry and you will make
the best speech you will ever regret.
Ambrose Bierce

Getting angry can sometimes be like leaping into a
wonderfully responsive sports car, gunning the motor,
taking off at high speed and then discovering
the brakes are out of order.
Maggie Scarf

To rule one's anger is well; to prevent it is still better.
Tyron Edwards

If you are patient in one moment of anger,
you will escape a hundred days of sorrow.
Chinese saying

It is impossible for you to be angry and laugh at the same time.
Anger and laughter are mutually exclusive
and you have the power to choose either.
Wayne Dyer

There are two ways of meeting difficulties:
you alter the difficulties, or you alter yourself
to meet them.
Phyllis Bottome

We win half the battle when we make up our minds to take
the world as we find it, including the thorns.
Orison S. Marden

Drag your thoughts away from your troubles—by the ears,
by the heels, or any other way you can manage it.
It's the healthiest thing a body can do.
Mark Twain

When the first Superman movie came out I was
frequently asked "What is a hero?"...My answer was that a hero
is someone who commits a courageous action
without considering the consequences....Now my definition is
completely different. I think a hero is an ordinary individual who finds
strength to persevere and endure in spite of overwhelming obstacles.
Christopher Reeve

The happy and efficient people in this world are those who
accept trouble as a normal detail of human life and resolve
to capitalize it when it comes along.
H. Bertram Lewis

Problems are only opportunities in work clothes.
Henry J. Kaiser

You seek problems because you need their gifts.
Richard Bach

Everything that irritates us about others
can lead us to an understanding of ourselves.
Carl Jung

Heartbreak is life educating us.
George Bernard Shaw

I learned long ago never to wrestle with a pig.
You get dirty, and besides, the pig likes it.
Cyrus Ching

When things are bad, we take comfort in the thought that
they could always be worse. And when they are,
we find hope in the thought that things are so bad
they have to get better.
Malcolm Forbes

When I hear somebody sigh, "Life is hard,"
I am always tempted to ask, "Compared to what?"
Sydney J. Harris

When life's problems seem overwhelming, look around
and see what other people are coping with.
You may consider yourself fortunate.
Ann Landers

When you dig another out of their troubles,
you find a place to bury your own.
Anonymous

The human capacity to fight back will always astonish
doctors and philosophers. It seems, indeed, that there are no
circumstances so bad and no obstacles so big
that man cannot conquer them.
Jean Tetreau

The bitterest misfortune can be covered up with a smile.
Yiddish folk saying

He knows not his own strength that hath not met adversity.
Ben Jonson

Without adversity, without change, life is boring.
The paradox of comfort is that we stop trying.
John Amatt

Take chances, make mistakes. That's how you grow.
Pain nourishes your courage.
You have to fail in order to practice being brave.
Mary Tyler Moore

Although the world is full of suffering,
it is also full of the overcoming of it.
Helen Keller

You Don't Have to Suffer
Judy Tatelbaum

One of the secrets of life is to make stepping stones
out of stumbling blocks.
Jack Penn

The worst thing in your life may contain seeds of the best.
When you can see crisis as an opportunity,
your life becomes not easier, but more satisfying.
Joe Kogel

What is to give light must endure burning.
Viktor Frankl

If we had no winter, the spring would not be so pleasant.
If we did not sometimes taste of adversity,
prosperity would not be so welcome.
Anne Bradstreet

He who can't endure the bad will not live
to see the good.
Yiddish saying

The way I see it, if you want the rainbow,
you gotta put up with the rain.
Dolly Parton

If we fight against the waves that pass over us in life, we are overpowered. If we move with the waves in life as they roll over us, the wave passes on.
Pesikta Zurtarti

Expect trouble as an inevitable part of life and repeat to yourself the most comforting words of all: This, too, shall pass.
Ann Landers

change & challenge

change *v* to cause to be different

chal•lenge *n* a test of one's abilities in a demanding undertaking

---

It's always something.
Gilda Radner

There is nothing permanent except change.
Heraclitus

Everything is changing.
People are taking their comedians seriously
and the politicians as a joke.
Will Rogers

The more things change, the more they remain the same.
Alphonse Karr

Even if you're on the right track,
you'll get run over if you just sit there.
Will Rogers

It seems necessary to completely shed the old skin
before the new, brighter, stronger, more beautiful one
can emerge....I never thought I'd be getting
a life lesson from a snake.
Julie Ridge

Should you shield the canyons from the windstorms,
you would never see the beauty of their carvings.
Elisabeth Kübler-Ross

To keep our faces toward change and behave like free
spirits in the presence of fate is strength undefeatable.
Helen Keller

Happy is he who learns to bear what he cannot change.
J. C. F. von Schiller

If matters go badly now,
they will not always do so.
Horace

Perhaps one day this too will be pleasant to remember.
Virgil

This, too, shall pass.
William Shakespeare

In spite of illness, in spite even of the archenemy sorrow,
one can remain alive long past the usual date
of disintegration if one is unafraid of change,
insatiable in intellectual curiosity, interested in big things,
and happy in small ways.
Edith Wharton

Changes are not only possible and predictable,
but to deny them is to be an accomplice
to one's own unnecessary vegetation.
Gail Sheehy

We cannot change anything unless we accept it.
Carl Jung

If you can't change your fate, change your attitude.
Amy Tan

A positive attitude may not solve all your problems, but it will
annoy enough people to make it worth the effort.
Herm Albright

Life is change. Growth is optional. Choose wisely.
Karen Kaiser Clark

When you're through changing, you're through.
Bruce Barton

If you realize that all things change,
there is nothing you will try to hold onto.
Tao Te Ching

A permanent state of transition
is man's most noble condition.
Juan Ramon Jimenez

Consistency is contrary to nature, contrary to life.
The only completely consistent people are the dead.
Aldous Huxley

If you fear change, leave it here.
Sign on a restaurant tip jar

You learn more from ten days of agony
than from ten years of content.
Sally Jessy Raphael

So often we try to alter circumstances to suit ourselves,
instead of letting them alter us,
which is what they are meant to do.
Mother Maribel

I have always grown from my problems and challenges,
from things that don't work out;
that's when I've really learned.
Carol Burnett

The hardships of life are sent not by an unkind
destiny to crush, but to challenge.
Sam E. Roberts

The ultimate measure of a man is not where he stands in
moments of comfort and convenience, but where he stands
at times of challenge and controversy.
Martin Luther King, Jr.

Sometimes things which at the moment may be
perceived as obstacles—and actually be obstacles,
difficulties, or drawbacks—can in the long run result
in some good end which would not have occurred
if it had not been for the obstacle.
Steve Allen

God gave burdens, also shoulders.
Yiddish saying

That which does not kill me makes me stronger.
Friedrich Nietzsche

We all have to go through the tumbler a few times
before we can emerge as a crystal.
Elisabeth Kübler Ross

The gem cannot be polished without friction,
nor man perfected without trials.
Chinese saying

Everyone gets their rough day. No one gets a free ride.
Today so far, I had a good day. I got a dial tone.
Rodney Dangerfield

I have seen what a laugh can do. It can transform almost
unbearable tears into something bearable, even hopeful.
Bob Hope

One of the things I learned the hard way was
that it doesn't pay to get discouraged. Keeping
busy and making optimism a way of life can restore
your faith in yourself.
Lucille Ball

I have never been disabled in my dreams.
Christopher Reeve

Keep your face to the sunshine
and you cannot see the shadow.
Helen Keller

The "crisis" of yesterday is the joke of tomorrow.
H. G. Wells

**dating, marriage
& divorce
death & dying
diet & exercise**

dat•ing *v* to go on a date with

mar•riage *n* legal union of a man and woman as husband and wife

di•vorce *n* legal dissolution of a marriage

When you're first single, you're so optimistic.
At the beginning, you're like: "I want to meet a guy who's really
smart, really sweet, really good-looking, has a really
great career."...Six months later, you're like:
"Lord—any mammal with a day job."
Carol Leifer

I was out on a date recently and the guy took
me horseback riding. That was kind of fun, until we
ran out of quarters.
Susie Loucks

Do you know the best way for a guy to impress a girl at the gym?
The best way is to do pull-ups...pull up in a Corvette, pull up in
a Rolls-Royce, pull up in a Cadillac.
Conan O'Brien

When I'm dating I look at a guy and wonder, "Is this the man I want my
children to spend their weekends with?"
Rita Rudner

Let's face it, a date is like a job interview that lasts all night. The only difference between the two is that there are very few job interviews where there's a chance you will end up naked at the end of it.

Jerry Seinfeld

Personally, I think if a woman hasn't met the right man
by the time she's 24, she may be lucky.

Deborah Kerr

A girl can wait for the right man to come along
but in the meantime that still doesn't mean she can't have
a wonderful time with all the wrong ones.

Cher

I just broke up with someone and the last thing she said to me was,
"You'll never find anyone like me again!"
I'm thinking, "I should hope not! If I don't want you,
why would I want someone like you?"

Larry Miller

My boyfriend and I broke up.
He wanted to get married and I didn't want him to.

Rita Rudner

Marriage is a great institution,
but I'm not ready for an institution yet.
Mae West

In Hollywood a marriage is a success if it outlasts milk.
Rita Rudner

Marriage is the alliance of two people,
one of whom never remembers birthdays
and the other never forgets them.
Ogden Nash

Marriage is not just spiritual communion and passionate embraces;
marriage is also three-meals-a-day
and remembering to carry out the trash.
Joyce Brothers

A successful marriage requires falling in love many times,
always with the same person.
Mignon McLaughlin

If marriage is your object,
you'd better start loving your subject.
Anonymous

All marriages are happy.
It's trying to live together afterwards
that causes all the problems.
Shelley Winters

There's only one way to have a happy marriage
and as soon as I learn what is it I'll get married again.
Clinton Eastwood

I'd marry again if I found a man who had
fifteen million dollars, would sign over half to me,
and guarantee that he'd be dead within a year.
Bette Davis

An archeologist is the best husband a woman can have;
the older she gets, the more interested he is in her.
Agatha Christie

Husbands are like fires.
They go out if unattended.
Zsa Zsa Gabor

Only two things are necessary to keep one's wife happy.
One is to let her think she is having her own way,
and the other, to let her have it.
Lyndon B. Johnson

The best way to get most husbands to do something
is to suggest that perhaps they're too old to do it.
Shirley MacLaine

The reason husbands and wives do not understand each
other is because they belong to different sexes.
Dorothy Dix

Marrying a man is like buying something you've been
admiring for a long time in a shop window.
You may love it when you get it home,
but it doesn't always go with everything else.
Jean Kerr

My parents want me to get married.
They don't care who anymore as long as he doesn't have
a pierced ear, that's all they care about. I think men who
have a pierced ear are better prepared for marriage.
They've experienced pain and bought jewelry.
Rita Rudner

I've always said we got married
because there was nothing on TV.
Bette Midler

Getting divorced just because you don't love a man
is almost as silly as getting married just because you do.
Zsa Zsa Gabor

It wasn't exactly a divorce—I was traded.
Tim Conway

I've never married, but I tell people I'm divorced
so they won't think something's wrong with me.
Elayne Boosler

Divorce: A fifty-fifty settlement of the property, where one
gets the house and the other gets the mortgage.
Evan Esar

In Hollywood, an equitable divorce settlement means
each party getting fifty percent of publicity.
Lauren Bacall

One reason people get divorced
is that they run out of gift ideas.
Robert Byrne

Being divorced is like being hit by a Mack
truck—if you survive you start looking very carefully
to the right and left.
Jean Kerr

For a while, we pondered whether
to take a vacation or get a divorce.
We decided that a trip to Bermuda is over in two weeks,
but a divorce is something you always have.
Woody Allen

That's the only good thing about divorce.
You get to sleep with your mother.
Anita Loos

death *n*   termination of life

dy•ing *v*   to cease living

It matters not how a man dies, but how he lives.
Samuel Johnson

The value of life lies not in the length of days,
but in the use we make of them;
a man may live long yet live very little.
Montaigne

Death is not the greatest loss in life.
The greatest loss is what dies inside us while we live.
Norman Cousins

Let us so live that when we come to die
even the undertaker will be sorry.
Mark Twain

There are worse things in life than death.
Have you ever spent an evening
with an insurance salesman?
Woody Allen

Death: Nature's way of making you slow down.
Evan Esar

Death is nature's way of saying your table is ready.
Robin Williams

Death is nothing to fear. It is only another dimension.
Wayne Dyer

Death is simply a shedding of the physical body,
like the butterfly coming out of a cocoon....
It's like putting away your winter coat
when spring comes.
Elisabeth Kübler-Ross

When one man dies, one chapter is not torn out of the
book, but translated into a better language.
John Donne

One of the situations in which everybody seems to fear
loneliness is death. In tones drenched with pity,
people say of someone, "He died alone."
I have never understood this point of view.
Who wants to have to die and be polite at
the same time?
Quentin Crisp

It's not that I'm afraid to die,
I just don't want to be there when it happens.
Woody Allen

If my doctor told me I only had six minutes to live,
I wouldn't brood. I'd type a little faster.
Isaac Asimov

If you bemoan your brief stay on earth,
consider the mayfly which lives only for one day.
If the weather were bad that day,
your whole life could be rained out.
Wes "Scoop" Nisker

Everybody wants to go to heaven,
but nobody wants to die.
Joe Louis

Losing is the price we pay for living.
It is also the source of much of our growth and gain.
Judith Viorst

I think the most you can hope for at the end of life is that
your hair's messed, you're out of breath,
and you didn't throw up.
Jerry Seinfeld

We find by losing. We hold fast by letting go.
We become something new by ceasing to be something
old. This seems to be close to the heart of that mystery.
I know no more now than I ever did about the far side of
death as the last letting-go of all, but now I know that I do
not need to know, and that I do not need to be afraid of
not knowing. God knows. That is all that matters.

Frederick Buechner

To live in hearts we leave behind
Is not to die.

Thomas Campbell

The highest tribute to the dead is not grief but gratitude.

Thornton Wilder

To weep too much for the dead is to affront the living.

Old saying

Weeping may endure for a night,
but joy cometh in the morning.

Psalms 30:5

It is foolish to tear one's hair in grief,
as though sorrow would be made less by baldness.

Cicero

We learn as much from sorrow as from joy,
as much from illness as from health, from handicap as
from advantage—and indeed perhaps more.

Pearl S. Buck

If life must not be taken too seriously—
then so neither must death.

Samuel Butler

Life does not cease to be funny when people die
any more than it ceases to be serious when people laugh.

George Bernard Shaw

I mean that's what death is really, it's the last big move of
your life. The hearse is like the van, the pallbearers are
your close friends, the only ones you could really ask to
help you with a big move like that. And the casket is that
great, perfect box you've been looking for your whole life.
The only problem is once you find it, you're in it.

Jerry Seinfeld

For three days after death, hair and fingernails continue to
grow but phone calls taper off.

Johnny Carson

Of all the deathbed regrets that I have heard
not one of them has been,
"I wish I had spent more time at the office."

Wayne Dyer

Don't send me flowers when I die—give them to me now
so we can appreciate their beauty together!
C. Leslie Charles

They say such nice things about people at their funerals
that it makes me sad to realize that
I'm going to miss mine by just a few days.
Garrison Keillor

I did not attend his funeral,
but I wrote a nice letter saying I approved of it.
Mark Twain

They say you shouldn't say nothing
about the dead unless it's good.
He's dead. Good.
Moms Mabley

No matter how great a man is,
the size of his funeral usually depends on the weather.
Rosemary Clooney

No matter who you are,
you only get a little slice of the world.
Have you ever seen a hearse followed by a U Haul?
Billy Graham

The sight of a gravestone, weighty not only in its granite,
allows us perspective on problems as pressing as
burnt toast, taxes, and hay fever.
Harrowsmith Country Life

Of all escape mechanisms, death is the most efficient.
H. L. Mencken

Death will be a great relief. No more interviews.
Katharine Hepburn

I can't die yet...I'm booked!
George Burns

I am ready to meet my Maker.
Whether my Maker is prepared for the ordeal
of meeting me is another matter.
Winston Churchill

I believe in sex and death—
two experiences that come once in a lifetime.
Woody Allen

The only difference between sex and death is,
with death you can do it alone and nobody's going to
make fun of you.
Woody Allen

I do not believe in an afterlife,
although I am bringing a change of underwear.
Woody Allen

Eternity is a terrible thought.
I mean, where's it going to end?
Tom Stoppard

If you die in the elevator, be sure to push the UP button.
Sam Levenson

di•et *v*   to eat or drink according to a regulated system

ex•er•cise *n*   activity that requires physical or mental exertion

---

One should eat to live, not live to eat.
Molière

To lengthen thy Life, lessen thy meals.
Benjamin Franklin

Never eat more than you can lift.
Miss Piggy

Food is an important part of a balanced diet.
Fran Lebowitz

I prefer Hostess fruit pies to pop-up toaster tarts
because they don't require so much cooking.
Carrie Snow

The two biggest sellers in any bookstore
are the cookbooks and the diet books.
The cookbooks tell you how to prepare the food
and the diet books tell you how not to eat any of it.
Andy Rooney

This recipe is certainly silly.
It says to separate two eggs,
but it doesn't say how far to separate them.
Gracie Allen

Artichokes...are just plain annoying....
After all the trouble you go to, you get about as much actual
"food" out of eating an artichoke as you would
from licking thirty or forty postage stamps.
Have the shrimp cocktail instead.
Miss Piggy

I'm on a seafood diet. I see food and I eat it.
Anonymous

I told my doctor I get very tired when I go on a diet, so he gave me
pep pills. Know what happened? I ate faster.
Joe E. Lewis

I've been on a diet for two weeks
and all I've lost is two weeks.
Totie Fields

I've been on a constant diet for the last two decades.
I've lost a total of 789 pounds. By all accounts, I should
be hanging from a charm bracelet.
Erma Bombeck

Eat, drink, and be merry, for tomorrow we diet!
Anonymous

I never worry about diets.
The only carrots that interest me
are the number you get in a diamond.
Mae West

To feel "fit as a fiddle," you must tone down your middle.
Anonymous

It's rough to go through life with your contents looking as if
they settled during shipping!
Milton Berle

He who does not mind his belly,
will hardly mind anything else.
Samuel Johnson

When I buy cookies I just eat four and throw the rest away. But first I spray them with Raid so I won't dig them out of the garbage later. Be careful, though, because that Raid really doesn't taste that bad.

Janette Barber

I've decided that perhaps I'm bulimic
and just keep forgetting to purge.

Paula Poundstone

I did not become a vegetarian for my health.
I did it for the health of the chickens.

Isaac Beshevis Singer

Health food makes me sick.

Calvin Trillin

Old people shouldn't eat health food.
They need all the preservatives they can get.

Robert Orben

You do live longer with bran
but you spend the last fifteen years on the toilet.

Alan King

The sovereign invigorator of the body is exercise,
and of all the exercises walking is the best.
Thomas Jefferson

A vigorous five-mile walk will do more good for an
unhappy but otherwise healthy adult than all the
medicine and psychology in the world.
Paul Dudley White

I like long walks,
especially when they are taken by people
who annoy me.
Fred Allen

My grandmother, she started walking five miles a day
when she was sixty. She's ninety-seven today—
we don't know where the hell she is.
Ellen Degeneres

You can't lose weight without exercise.
But I've got a philosophy about exercise.
I don't think you should punish your legs
for something your mouth did.
Drag your lips around the block once or twice.
Gwen Owen

The only reason I would take up jogging
is so I could hear heavy breathing again.
Erma Bombeck

I have never taken any exercise
except sleeping and resting.
Mark Twain

When I feel like exercising
I just lie down until the feeling goes away.
Robert M. Hutchins

A bear, however hard he tries,
grows tubby without exercise.
Pooh's Little Instruction Book,
inspired by A. A. Milne

I've been doing leg lifts faithfully for about fifteen years,
and the only thing that has gotten thinner is the carpet
where I have been doing the leg lifts.
Rita Rudner

Too many people confine their exercise to
jumping to conclusions, running up bills, stretching the truth,
bending over backward, lying down on the job,
sidestepping responsibility and pushing their luck.
Anonymous

I joined a health spa recently.
They had a sign for "Free Weights."
So I took a couple.
Scott Wood

Physical fitness is in.
I recently had a physical fit myself.
Steve Allen

friends & family

friends *n* people who one knows; acquaintances

fam•i•ly *n* a group of persons sharing common ancestry or goals

---

The only way to have a friend
is to be one.
Ralph Waldo Emerson

A man, Sir, should keep his friendship in constant repair.
Samuel Johnson

The best way to keep your friends
is not to give them away.
Wilson Mizner

The best time to make friends is before you need them.
Ethel Barrymore

Trouble is a sieve through which
we sift our acquaintances.
Those too big to pass through are our friends.
Arlene Francis

The essence of true friendship is
to make allowances for another's little lapses.
David Storey

A friend is a person who likes you for what you are,
in spite of all your faults, all your shortcomings.
Alfred Armand Montapert

In prosperity, our friends know us;
in adversity, we know our friends.
John Churton Collins

Lots of people want to ride with you in the limo,
but what you want is someone
who will take the bus with you
when the limo breaks down.
Oprah Winfrey

A friend is someone who allows you distance
but is never far away.
Noah benShea

A true friend is someone who is there for you
when he'd rather be anywhere else.
Len Wein

True friendship is seen through the heart
not through the eyes.

Anonymous

If you are looking for a friend who has no faults,
you will have no friends.

Hasidic folk saying

Laughter is not at all a bad beginning for a friendship,
and it is far the best ending for one.

Oscar Wilde

The most valuable things in life
are not measured in monetary terms.
The really important things are not
houses and lands, stocks and bonds,
automobiles and real estate,
but friendships, trust, confidence,
empathy, mercy, love and faith.

Bertrand Russell V. Delong

The holy passion of friendship is of so sweet and steady
and loyal and enduring a nature that it will last through a
whole lifetime, if not asked to lend money.

Mark Twain

A friend costs nothing.
An enemy you must pay for.
Yiddish folk saying

A friend is a person who had the same
enemies you have.
Stephen Leacock

A friend may well be reckoned
the masterpiece of Nature.
Ralph Waldo Emerson

Friendships multiply joy and divide griefs.
H. G. Bohn

My friends are my estate.
Emily Dickinson

A faithful friend is the medicine of life.
Ecclesiastes 6:16

True friendship is like sound health,
the value of it is seldom known until it be lost.
Charles Caleb Colton

Show me a genuine case of platonic friendship,
and I shall show you two old or homely faces.
Austin O'Malley

Each friend represents a world in us,
a world possibly not born until they arrive,
and it is only by this meeting that a new world is born.
Anais Nin

Life's truest happiness is found
in friendships we make along the way.
Anonymous

The happiest business in all the world
is that of making friends,
And no investment on the street
pays larger dividends,
For life is more than stocks and bonds,
and love than rate percent,
And he who gives in friendship's name
shall reap what he has spent.
Anonymous

There are three kinds of friends:
best friends, guest friends, and pest friends.
Laurence J. Peter

Man has three friends on whose company he relies.
First, wealth which goes with him only while good fortune
lasts. Second, his relatives; they go only as far as the
grave, leave him there. The third friend, his good deeds,
go with him beyond the grave.
The Talmud

Friendship with oneself is all important, because without it
one cannot be friends with anyone else in the world.
Eleanor Roosevelt

A home-made friend wears longer
than one you buy in the market.
Austin O'Malley

Think where man's glory most begins and ends,
And say my glory was I had such friends.
William Butler Yeats

Two are better than one, for if they fall,
the one will lift up his fellow.
Ecclesiastes 4:9–10

We are each of us angels with only one wing,
and we can only fly by embracing one another.
Luciano de Crescenzo

When a friend is in trouble, don't annoy him by asking
if there is anything you can do.
Think up something appropriate and do it.
Edgar Watson Howe

But friendship is precious, not only in the shade, but in the
sunshine of life; and thanks to a benevolent arrangement
of things, the greater part of life is sunshine.
Thomas Jefferson

False friendship, like the ivy, decays and ruins
the walls it embraces; but true friendship gives new life
and animation to the object it supports.
Richard Burton

No man is useless while he has a friend.
Robert Louis Stevenson

We need old friends to help us grow old
and new friends to help us stay young.
Letty Cotton Pogrebin

In everyone's life, at some time, our inner fire goes out.
It is then burst into flame by an encounter with another
human being. We should all be thankful
for those people who rekindle the inner spirit.
Albert Schweitzer

One loyal friend is worth ten thousand relatives.
Euripides

God gives us our relatives—
thank God we can choose our friends.
Ethel Watts Mumford

The family is one of nature's masterpieces.
George Santayana

Family: A social unit where the father is concerned
with parking space, the children with outer space,
and the mother with closet space.
Evan Esar

A family is a unit composed not only of children
but of men, women, an occasional animal,
and the common cold.
Ogden Nash

If you cannot get rid of the family skeleton,
you may as well make it dance.
George Bernard Shaw

The family you come from isn't as important
as the family you're going to have.
Ring Lardner

Happiness is having a large, loving, caring, close-knit
family in another city.
George Burns

My mother loved children—
she would have given anything if I had been one.
Groucho Marx

Mother, food, love, and career,
the four major guilt groups.
Cathy Guiswite

The most remarkable thing about my mother is that for
thirty years she served the family nothing but leftovers.
The original meal has never been found.
Calvin Trillin

God could not be everywhere,
so He created mothers.
Leopold Kompert

I have found that no kisses can ever compare
to "mom" kisses, because mom kisses can heal anything.
You can have a hangnail, a broken heart, or catatonic
schizophrenia; with moms, one kiss and you're fine.
Robert G. Lee

health & healing
housekeeping

health *n*   freedom from disease or abnormality

heal•ing *v*   to restore to health

The secret of health for both mind and body
is not to mourn for the past, nor to worry about the future,
but to live the present moment wisely and earnestly.
Buddha

To be healthy, wealthy, happy and successful in any and
all areas of your life you need to be aware that you need
to think healthy, wealthy, happy and successful thoughts
twenty-four hours a day and cancel all negative,
destructive, fearful and unhappy thoughts. These two types
of thought cannot coexist if you want to share in the
abundance that surrounds us all.
Sidney Madwed

Forgiveness is the way to true health and happiness.
Gerald Jampolsky

Forgiveness is all-powerful. Forgiveness heals all ills.
Catherine Ponder

Always forgive your enemies;
nothing annoys them so much.
Oscar Wilde

The healthy, the strong individual,
is the one who asks for help when he needs it.
Whether he has an abscess on his knee or in his soul.
Rona Barrett

The best and most efficient pharmacy
is within your own system.
Robert C. Peale

You don't get ulcers from what you eat.
You get them from what's eating you.
Vicki Baum

Be careful about reading health books.
You may die of a misprint.
Mark Twain

It's no longer a question of staying healthy.
It's a question of finding a sickness you like.
Jackie Mason

He's turned his life around.
He used to be depressed and miserable.
Now he's miserable and depressed.
David Frost

I moved to New York City for my health.
I'm paranoid and New York was the only place
where my fears were justified.
Anita Weiss

When we hate our enemies, we are giving them
power over us: power over our sleep, our appetites,
our blood pressure, our health, and our happiness.
Our enemies would dance with joy if only they knew how
they were worrying us, lacerating us, and getting even
with us! Our hate is not hurting them at all, but our hate
is turning our days and nights into a hellish turmoil.
Dale Carnegie

There's a lot of people in this world
who spend so much time watching their health
that they haven't the time to enjoy it.
Josh Billings

Health is the condition of wisdom,
and the sign is cheerfulness,
—an open and noble temper.
Ralph Waldo Emerson

The simple truth is
that happy people generally don't get sick.
Bernie S. Siegel

The body is the soul's house. Shouldn't we therefore take
care of our house so that it doesn't fall into ruin?
Philo

A man too busy to take care of his health
is like a mechanic too busy to take care of his tools.
Spanish saying

If I'd known I was going to live this long,
I'd have taken better care of myself.
Jimmy Durante

Joy, temperance, and repose, Slam the door on the doctor's nose.
Henry Wadsworth Longfellow

Wondrous is the strength of cheerfulness,
and its power of endurance—
the cheerful man will do more in the same time,
will do it better, will preserve it longer,
than the sad or sullen.
Thomas Carlyle

If your capacity to acquire has outstripped your capacity
to enjoy, you are on the way to the scrap-heap.
Glen Buck

Healing in its fullest sense requires looking into our heart
and expanding our awareness of who we are.
Mitchell Gaynor

When praying for healing, ask great things of God
and expect great things from God.
But let us seek for that healing that really matters,
the healing of the heart, enabling us to trust God simply,
face God honestly, and live triumphantly.
Arlo F. Newell

Our greatest healer is sitting right under our nose,
moving in and out—our breath.
Jacquelyn Small

The greatest secret of doctors, known only to their
wives, but still hidden from the public, is that
most things get better by themselves; most things,
in fact, are better in the morning.
Lewis Thomas

The greatest healing therapy is friendship and love.
Hubert Humphrey

The mind is its own place, and in itself,
can make heaven of Hell, and a hell of Heaven.
John Milton

What your mind possesses your body expresses.
Anonymous

When an emotional injury takes place, the body begins a
process as natural as the healing of a physical wound. Let
the process happen. Trust that nature will do the healing.
Know that the pain will pass and, when it passes, you will
be stronger, happier, more sensitive and aware.
Melba Colgrove, Harold H. Bloomfield & Peter McWilliams

No day is so bad it can't be fixed with a nap.
Carrie Snow

There must be quite a few things a hot bath won't cure,
but I don't know many of them.
Sylvia Plath

The power to heal is in you,
and nonetheless there is a tendency in our culture
to project onto other people and to want them to heal us.
Andrew Weil

Never go to a doctor whose office plants have died.
Erma Bombeck

My doctor said I look like a million dollars—
green and wrinkled.
Red Skelton

Some people think that doctors and nurses
can put scrambled eggs back into the shell.
Dorothy Canfield Fisher

A rule of thumb in the matter of medical advice
is to take everything any doctor says
with a grain of aspirin.
Goodman Ace

house•keep•ing *n* performance of household tasks

I hate housework! You make the beds, you do the dishes; and six
months later you have to start all over again.
Joan Rivers

Cleaning your house while your kids are still growing
is like shoveling the walk before it stops snowing.
Phyllis Diller

The darn trouble with cleaning the house is
it gets dirty the next day anyway, so skip a week if you have to.
The children are the most important thing.
Barbara Bush

There is no need to do any housework at all.
After the first four years the dirt doesn't get any worse.
Quentin Crisp

I would rather lie on a sofa than sweep beneath it.
Shirley Conran

The Rose Bowl is the only bowl I've ever seen
that I didn't have to clean.
Erma Bombeck

I'm a housewife. I'm not going to vacuum
'til Sears makes one you can ride on.
Roseanne

The toughest thing about being a housewife is
you have no place to stay home from.
Patricia C. Beudoin

I'm a great housekeeper.
I get divorced, I keep the house.
Zsa Zsa Gabor

Rich people do spring cleaning too.
Liz Taylor is completely exhausted after
spraying Windex on her diamonds.
Karen Lee

Thank God for dirty dishes;
they have a tale to tell.
While other folks go hungry,
we're eating pretty well.
With home, and health, and happiness,
we shouldn't want to fuss;
For by this stack of evidence,
God's very good to us.
Anonymous

There is such a build-up of crud in my oven
there is only room to bake a single cupcake.
Phyllis Diller

I can't cook. I use a smoke alarm as a timer.
Carol Siskind

I tried to save grocery money once, but some of the
suggestions were just not practical, like
"Don't shop when you're hungry,"
which eliminated all hours when the store was open.
Erma Bombeck

Be it ever so humble, there's no place like home.
John Howard Payne

A good laugh is sunshine in a house.
William Makepeace Thackeray

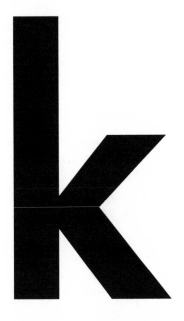

kids

ba•bies *n* a very young child; an infant

chil•dren *n* a person between birth and puberty

teen•ag•ers *n* a person between ages 13 and 19

———————

Babies are such a nice way to start people.
Don Herold

A baby is God's opinion that the world should go on.
Carl Sandburg

When you are a mother, you are never really alone
in your thoughts. A mother always has to think twice,
once for herself and once for her child.
Sophia Loren

Making the decision to have a child—it's wondrous.
It is to decide forever to have your heart
go walking around outside your body.
Elizabeth Stone

It sometimes happens, even in the best of families, that a
baby is born. This is not necessarily cause for alarm.
The important thing is to keep your wits about you
and borrow some money.
Elinor Goulding Smith

Life is a flame that is always burning itself out,
but it catches fire again ever time a child is born.
George Bernard Shaw

When the first baby laughed for the first time, the laugh
broke into a thousand pieces and they all went skipping
about, and that was the beginning of fairies.
J. M. Barrie

Somewhere on this globe every ten seconds,
there is a woman giving birth to a child.
She must be found and stopped.
Sam Levenson

[On pregnancy] To me, life is tough enough
without having someone kick you from the inside.
Rita Rudner

It takes the whole village to raise the child.
African Saying

Before I got married I had six theories about bringing up
children; now I have six children and no theories.
Lord Rochester

A child is a curly, dimpled lunatic.
Ralph Waldo Emerson

Raising children is a creative endeavor,
an art, rather than a science.
Bruno Bettelheim

In automobile terms, the child supplies the power
but the parents have to do the steering.
Benjamin Spock

A child is the greatest poem ever known.
Christopher Morley

Pretty much all the honest truth telling there is in the world
is done by children.
Oliver Wendell Holmes

While we try to teach our children all about life,
our children teach us what life is all about.
Angela Schwindt

Seek the wisdom of the ages,
but look at the world through the eyes of a child.
Ron Wild

There are children playing in the streets who could solve
some of my top problems in physics, because they have
modes of sensory perception that I lost long ago.
J. Robert Oppenheimer

You don't know how much you don't know
until your children grow up and tell you
how much you don't know.
S. J. Perelman

Children ask better questions than adults.
"May I have a cookie?" "Why is the sky blue?" and
"What does a cow say?" are far more likely to elicit a
cheerful response than "Where's your manuscript?" "Why
haven't you called?" and "Who's your lawyer?"
Fran Lebowitz

Hang around doggies and kids;
they know how to play.
Geoffrey Godbey

Parents learn a lot from their children
about coping with life.
Muriel Spark

You can learn many things from children.
How much patience you have, for instance.
Franklin P. Jones

Remember, when they have a tantrum,
don't have one of your own.
Judith Kuriensky

If you listen carefully to children
you will have plenty about which to laugh.
Steve Allen

Children have more need of models than of critics.
Joseph Joubert

If I could say just one thing to parents, it would be simply
that a child needs someone who believes in him
no matter what he does.
Alice Keliher

Never fear spoiling children by making them too happy.
Happiness is the atmosphere
in which all good affections grow.
Ann Eliza Bray

The word no carries a lot more meaning when spoken by
a parent who also knows how to say yes.
Joyce Maynard

The words that a father speaks to his children in the
privacy of home are not heard by the world, but,
as in whispering-galleries, they are clearly
heard at the end and by posterity.
Jean Paul Richter

If you want children to improve, let them overhear
the nice things you say about them to others.
Haim Ginott

Most kids hear what you say;
some kids do what you say;
but all kids do what you do.
Kathleen Casey Theisa

If a child is to keep alive his inborn sense of wonder
without any such gilt from the fairies, he needs the
companionship of at least one adult who can share it,
rediscovering with him the joy, excitement and mystery of
the world we live in.
Rachel Carson

The best thing to spend on your children is your time.
Louise Hart

To help your children turn out well,
spend twice as much time with them
and half as much money.
H. Jackson Brown

Children in a family are like flowers in a bouquet;
there's always one determined to face in an opposite
direction from the way the arranger desires.
Marcelene Cox

Likely as not, the child you can do the least with
will do the most to make you proud.
Mignon McLaughlin

The way we know our kids are growing up:
The bite marks are higher.
Phyllis Diller

There are times when parenthood seems nothing but
feeding the mouth that bites you.
Peter De Vries

I take my children everywhere;
but they always seem to find their way back home.
Robert Orben

We've had bad luck with our kids—they've all grown up.
Christopher Morley

The quickest way for a parent to get a child's attention
is to sit down and look comfortable.
Lan Olinghouse

The best way to keep children home is to make the home
atmosphere pleasant—and let the air out of the tires.
Dorothy Parker

It goes without saying that you should never have
more children than you have car windows.
Erma Bombeck

Never lend your car to anyone
to whom you have given birth.
Erma Bombeck

Anyone who thinks that art of conversation is dead
ought to tell a child to go to bed.
Robert Gallagher

Any kid will run an errand for you,
if you ask him at bedtime.
Red Skelton

I have found the best way to give advice
to your children is to find out what they want
and then advise them to do it.
Harry S Truman

The easiest way to convince my kids that they don't really
need something is to get it for them.
Joan Collins

Grandchildren are God's way
of compensating us for growing old.
Mary H. Waldrip

Be nice to your kids. They choose your nursing home.
Bumper sticker

Adolescence is like cactus.
Anais Nin

Adolescence is that period in kids' lives
when their parents become more difficult.
Ryan O' Neal

There's nothing wrong with teenagers
that reasoning with them won't aggravate.
Anonymous

The teenagers ain't all bad. I love 'em if nobody else does.
There ain't nothin' wrong with young people.
Jus' quit lyin' to 'em.
Moms Mabley

Teenagers travel in droves, packs swarms....
To the librarian, they're a gaggle of geese.
To the cook, they're a scourge of locusts.
To department stores they're a big beautiful
exaltation of larks...
all lovely and loose and jingly.
Bernice Fitz-Gibbon

Remember that as a teenager you are at the last stage
in your life when you will be happy to hear
that the phone is for you.
Fran Lebowitz

Teenagers are hormones with feet.
Marsha Doble

life & living

life *n*   the state or condition of a living organism

liv•ing *n*   the condition or action of maintaining life

Life is all memory, except for the one present moment
that goes by you so quickly you hardly catch it going.
Tennessee Williams

Life isn't a matter of milestones, but of moments.
Rose Kennedy

I am beginning to learn that it is the sweet, simple things
of life which are the real ones after all.
Laura Ingalls Wilder

Sooner or later we all discover that the important moments
in life are not the advertised ones, not the birthdays, the
graduations, the weddings, not the great goals achieved.
The real milestones are less prepossessing. They come to
the door of memory unannounced, stray dogs that amble
in, sniff around a bit, and simply never leave.
Our lives are measured by these.
Susan B. Anthony

If I had my life to live over again...I would have
more actual troubles and less imaginary ones.
Oh, I've had my moments, and if I had to do it over
again, I'd have more of them. In fact, I'd try to have
nothing else, just moments, one after another.

Nadine Stair

If I had to live my life again,
I'd make the same mistakes, only sooner.

Tallulah Bankhead

If I had my life to live over,
I'd live over a delicatessen.

Anonymous

Life is like a box of chocolates.

Forrest Gump

Life is too short to stuff a mushroom.

Shirley Conran

Life is better than death, I believe, if only because
it is less boring, and because it has fresh peaches in it.

Alice Walker

Life is far too important a thing
ever to talk seriously about.

Oscar Wilde

Not a shred of evidence exists in favor of the idea
that life is serious.
Brendan Gill

Life is too tragic for sadness.
Let us rejoice.
Edward Abbey

In every moment, the quality of your life is on the line.
In each, you are either fully alive or relatively dead.
Dan Millman

Life is no brief candle to me. It is a sort of
splendid torch which I've got hold of for the moment
and I want to make it burn as brightly as possible
before handing it on to the future generations.
George Bernard Shaw

Life is not so bad if you have plenty of luck,
a good physique and not too much imagination.
Christopher Isherwood

Life is like a ten-speed bike.
Most of us have gears we never use.
Charles Schulz

Life is a great big canvas;
throw all the paint on it you can.
Danny Kaye

Life is like a blanket too short. You pull it up and
your toes rebel, you yank it down and shivers meander
about your shoulder; but cheerful folks manage to draw
their knees up and pass a very comfortable night.
Marion Howard

I am convinced that life is 10% what happens to me
and 90% how I react to it.
Charles Swindoll

Life is not the way it's supposed to be. It's the way it is.
The way you cope with it is what makes the difference.
Virginia Satir

Remember, life is not what happens to you
but what you make of what happens to you.
Everyone dies, but not everyone fully lives.
Too many people are having "near-life experiences."
Anonymous

I think of life itself, now, as a wonderful play
that I've written for myself....And so my purpose is
to have the most fun playing my part.
Shirley MacLaine

If you're too busy to enjoy life, you're too busy.
Jeff Davidson

Do not take life too seriously.
You will never get out of it alive.
Elbert Hubbard

All I can say about life is, Oh God, enjoy it!
Bob Newhart

Life is a jest; and all things show it.
I thought so once; but now I know it.
John Gay

Be glad of life because it gives you the chance to love,
and to work, and to play and to look up at the stars.
Henry Van Dyke

One should sympathize with the joy, the beauty, the color
of life—the less said about life's sores the better.
Oscar Wilde

So much sadness exists in the world
that we are all under obligation to contribute
as much joy as lies within our powers.
John Sutherland Bonnell

It's a funny thing about life;
if you refuse to accept anything but the best,
you very often get it.
W. Somerset Maugham

The happiness of your life depends
upon the quality of your thoughts.
Marcus Antonius

The greatest discovery of any generation is that human
beings can alter their lives by altering their attitudes.
Albert Schweitzer

I realized that if what we call human nature can be
changed, then absolutely anything is possible.
From that moment, my life changed.
Shirley MacLaine

The grand essentials to happiness in this life
are something to do, something to love
and something to hope for.
Joseph Addison

We act as though comfort and luxury were the chief
requirements of life, when all that we need to make us
really happy is something to be enthusiastic about.
Charles Kingsley

Life is a paradise for those who love
many things with a passion.
Leo Buscaglia

The secret of life is to have a task,
something you devote your entire life to,
something you bring everything to, ever minute of the day
for the rest of your life. And the most important thing is,
it must be something you cannot possibly do.
Henry Moore

I have very strong feelings about how you lead your life.
You always look ahead, you never look back.
Ann Richards

Living in the past is a dull and lonely business;
looking back strains the neck muscles,
causes you to bump into people not going your way.
Edna Ferber

Life is like playing a violin solo in public,
and learning the instrument as one goes on.
Samuel Butler

Life can only be understood backwards;
but it must be lived forwards.
Søren Kierkegaard

Nobody gets to live life backward.
Look ahead—that's where your future lies.
Ann Landers

The best way to prepare for life is to begin to live.
Elbert Hubbard

If you want my final opinion on the mystery
of life and all that, I can give it to you in
a nutshell. The universe is like a safe
to which there is a combination.
But the combination is locked up in the safe.
Peter De Vries

Life is the greatest of all bargains; you get it for nothing.
Yiddish saying

Life is something to do when you can't get to sleep.
Fran Lebowitz

Life would be infinitely happier if we could only be born at
the age of eighty and gradually approach eighteen.
Mark Twain

Life:
Another game that is played with cards:
post-, greeting, punch, and credit.
Evan Esar

The purpose of life is a life of purpose.
Robert Byrne

We make a living by what we get,
but we make a life by what we give.
Winston Churchill

Only a life lived for others is a life worthwhile.
Albert Einstein

When people are serving, life is no longer meaningless.
John Gardner

There must be more to life than having everything!
Maurice Sendak

The best advice I ever received was from a friend, who
once told me, "You can have anything you want.
You just can't have everything you want."
John-Roger & Peter McWilliams

The best advice I've ever received? How about the strangest?
When I was thirteen, my father took me aside and told me that all
a girl needed to know to get by in life was written on the top of a
mayonnaise jar. I puzzled for days about the meaning of the phrase,
"Refrigerate After Opening"—until my father remarked that in his day
mayo jars always said, "Keep Cool, Don't Freeze."
C. E. Crimmins

In three words I can sum up everything
I've learned about life. It goes on.
Robert Frost

Enjoy the little things in life, for one day you may look
back and realize they were the big things.
Anonymous

One of the secrets of a happy life
is continuous small treats.
Iris Murdoch

My advice to you is not to inquire why or whither,
but just enjoy your ice cream while it's on your plate.
Thornton Wilder

There are two things to aim at in life:
first, to get what you want; and, after that, to enjoy it.
Only the wisest of mankind achieve the second.
Logan Pearsall Smith

I finally figured out the only reason
to be alive is to enjoy it.
Rita Mae Brown

I don't want to get to the end of my life
and find that I lived just the length of it.
I want to have lived the width of it as well.
Diane Ackerman

Every day we should hear at least one little song,
read one good poem, see one exquisite picture, and,
if possible, speak a few sensible words.
Johann Wolfgang von Goethe

Don't be afraid to go out on a limb.
That's where the fruit is.
H. Jackson Brown

Life engenders life. Energy creates energy.
It is by spending oneself that one becomes rich.
Sarah Bernhardt

Look, I really don't want to wax philosophic, but
I will say that if you're alive, you got to flap your arms
and legs, you got to jump around a lot, you got to make a
lot of noise, because life is the very opposite of death.
And therefore, as I see it, if you're quiet, you're not living.
You've got to be noisy, or at least your thoughts should be
noisy and colorful and lively.
Mel Brooks

Live as if you expected to live a hundred years,
but might die tomorrow.
Ann Lee

Beginning today, treat everyone you meet
as if they were going to be dead by midnight.
Extend to them all the care, kindness and
understanding you can muster, and do with no thought
of any reward. Your life will never be the same again.
Og Mandino

There are two ways of spreading light:
to be the candle or the mirror that reflects it.
Edith Wharton

Most of the shadows of this life are caused by
our standing in our own sunshine.
Ralph Waldo Emerson

The world is a mirror: what looks in looks out.
It gives back only what you lend it.
Ludwig Boeme

The follies which a person regrets most in his life are those
he didn't commit when he had the opportunity.
Helen Rowland

Twenty years from now you will be more disappointed
by the things you didn't do than by the ones you did.
So throw off the bowlines. Sail away from the safe
harbor. Catch the trade winds in your sails.
Explore. Dream. Discover.

Mark Twain

First I was dying to finish high school and start college.
And then I was dying to finish college and start working.
And then I was dying to marry and have children
to grow old enough so I could return to work.
And then I was dying to retire. And now, I am dying...
and suddenly realize I forgot to live.

Anonymous

Live in such a way that you would not be ashamed to sell
your parrot to the town gossip.

Will Rogers

There are only two ways to live your life.
One is as though nothing is a miracle.
The other is as though everything is a miracle.

Albert Einstein

It's all a miracle.
I have adopted the technique of living life
from miracle to miracle.

Arthur Rubinstein

If we could see the miracle of a single flower clearly,
our whole life would change.
Buddha

The art of being happy lies in the power of
extracting happiness from common things.
Henry Ward Beecher

Anyone can be happy when times are good;
the richer experience is to be happy when times are not.
Susan Harris

All the wonderful things in life are so simple that one is not
aware of their wonder until they are beyond touch.
Frances Gunther

Lightness of touch and living in the moment are
intertwined. One cannot dance well unless one is
completely in time with the music,
not leaning back to the last step
or pressing forward to the next one,
but poised directly on the present step as it comes.
Anne Morrow Lindbergh

The moment you know how, you begin to die a little.
The artist never entirely knows. We guess. We may be wrong,
but we take leap after leap in the dark.
Agnes de Mille

We are not permitted to choose the frame of our destiny.
But what we put into it is ours.
Dag Hammarskjöld

You don't get to choose how you're going to die. Or when.
You can only decide how you're going to live. Now.
Joan Baez

Your only obligation in any lifetime is
to be true to yourself.
Richard Bach

Other people attempt to live their lives backwards;
they try to have more things or more money, in order
to do more of what they want, so they will be happier.
The way it actually works is the reverse. You must first
be who you really are, then do what you need to do,
in order to have what you want.
Margaret Mead

Think of all the beauty still left around you and be happy.
Anne Frank

There is nothing worse than being born
extraordinarily beautiful, nothing more potentially
damaging to the self. You could say the same for being
born inordinately rich. You suddenly realize how wise the idea is that
you get nothing at birth except things to transcend. That's all you get.

Milton Glaser

I didn't belong as a kid, and that always bothered me.
If only I'd known that one day my differentness
would be an asset, then my early life
would have been much easier.

Bette Midler

He who has the why to live
can bear with almost any how.

Friedrich Nietzsche

You are the creature of circumstance or the creator.

Cavett Robert

Getting born is like being given a ticket to the theatrical
event called life. It's like going to the theater. Now, all that
ticket will get you, is through the door. It doesn't get you a good time
and it doesn't get you a bad time. You go in and sit down and you
either love the show or you don't. If you do, terrific. And if you don't—
That's show business.

Stewart Emery

Don't wait around for other people to be happy for you. Any happiness you get you've got to make yourself.
Alice Walker

The last of human freedoms—to choose one's attitude in any given set of circumstances, to choose one's own way.
Victor Frankl

If you can spend a perfectly useless afternoon in a perfectly useless manner, you have learned how to live.
Lin Yutang

men & women
money matters

men *n* adult male human beings

wom•en *n* adult female human beings

What is most beautiful in virile men is something feminine;
what is most beautiful in feminine women
is something masculine.
Susan Sontag

The ideal man has the strength of a male
and the compassion of a female.
Zohar

Women speak because they wish to speak,
whereas a man speaks only when driven to speech
by something outside himself—
like for instance, he can't find any clean socks.
Jean Kerr

Every man who is high up likes to think he has done it all
himself; and the wife smiles, and lets it go at that.
It's our only joke. Every woman knows that.
J. M. Barrie

It's not the men in my life, but the life in my men.
Mae West

I never hated a man enough to give him diamonds back.
Zsa Zsa Gabor

If men can run the world, why can't they stop
wearing neckties? How intelligent is it to start the day
by tying a little noose around your neck?
Linda Ellerbee

Why are women wearing perfumes that smell
like flowers? Men don't like flowers. I've been
wearing a great scent.
It's called New Car Interior.
Rita Rudner

Give a man a fish and he has food for a day;
teach him how to fish and you can get rid of him
for the entire weekend.
Zenna Schaffer

Men aren't men until they can get to Sears by themselves.
Tim Allen

If a woman gets nervous, she'll eat or go shopping.
A man will attack a country—
it's a whole other way of thinking.
Elayne Boosler

Fighting is essentially a masculine idea;
a woman's weapon is her tongue.
Hermione Gingold

When men reach their sixties and retire, they go to pieces.
Women go right on cooking.
Gail Sheehy

Remember, Ginger Rogers did everything Fred Astaire did,
but she did it backwards and in high heels.
Faith Whittlesey

I hate women because
they always know where things are.
James Thurber

The people I'm furious with are the Women's Liberationists.
They keep getting up on soapboxes and proclaiming
women are brighter than men. That's true, but it should be
kept quiet or it ruins the whole racket.
Anita Loos

We women don't care too much about getting our pictures
on money as long as we can get our hands on it.
Ivy (Maude) Baker Priest

There's really nothing wrong with a woman welcoming all men's advances, darling, as long as they are in cash.
Zsa Zsa Gabor

I bank at a women's bank.
It's closed three or four days a month due to cramps.
Judy Carter

The trouble with some women is they get all excited about nothing—and then they marry him.
Cher

Women complain about sex more often than men.
Their gripes fall into two major categories:
(1) Not enough (2) Too much.
Ann Landers

Why does a woman work ten years to change a man's habits and then complain that he's not the man she married?
Barbra Streisand

The only time a woman really succeeds in changing a man is when he's a baby.
Natalie Wood

Show me a woman who doesn't feel guilty
and I'll show you a man.
Erica Jong

Sometimes I wonder if men and women really suit each other. Perhaps
they should live next door and just visit now and then.
Katharine Hepburn

Men and women, women and men. It will never work.
Erica Jong

mon•ey *n* official currency issued by a government

Money is better than poverty if only for financial reasons.
Woody Allen

Money is a good thing to have.
It frees you from doing things you dislike.
Since I dislike doing nearly everything, money is handy.
Groucho Marx

Money is relative...the more money that rolls in
the more the relatives.
Anonymous

Money talks all right. Usually it says, "Good-bye."
Anonymous

On income tax day I am reminded that while people say
money talks, mine seems to go without saying a word.
Mary Ellen Pinkham

I'm proud to pay taxes in the United States;
the only thing is, I could be just as proud
for half the money.
Arthur Godfrey

I believe we should all pay our tax bill with a smile.
I tried—but they wanted cash.
Anonymous

It is more blessed to give than to receive.
Acts 20:35

Not only is it more blessed to give than receive—
it is also deductible.
Anonymous

Money doesn't always bring happiness.
People with ten million dollars are no happier
than people with nine million dollars.
Hobart Brown

There's no reason to be the richest man in the cemetery.
You can't do any business from there.
Colonel Sanders

I didn't want to be rich.
I just wanted enough to get the couch reupholstered.
Kate (Mrs. Zero) Mostel

If you want to know how rich you really are,
find out what would be left of you tomorrow
if you should lose every dollar you own tonight.
W. J. Boetcker

Measure wealth not by the things you have,
but by the things you have for which
you would not take money.
Anonymous

The man is the richest whose pleasures are the cheapest.
Henry David Thoreau

The richest man in the world is not the one
who still has the first dollar he ever earned.
It's the man who still has his best friend.
Martha Mason

If you want an accounting of your worth,
count your friends.
Merry Browne

What's money?
A man is a success if he gets up in the morning
and goes to bed at night and in-between
does what he wants to do.
Bob Dylan

To fulfill a dream, to be allowed to sweat over lonely labor,
to be given a chance to create, is the meat and potatoes
of life. The money is gravy.
Bette Davis

Not he who has much is rich, but he who gives much.
Erich Fromm

None are so poor that they have nothing to give...
and none are so rich that they have nothing to receive.
Pope John Paul II

There is enough in the world for everyone's need,
but not enough for everyone's greed.
Frank Buchman

Money is like water. When water is moving
and flowing, it cleanses, it purifies, it makes things green,
it's beautiful. But when it starts to slow down and sludge,
it becomes toxic and stagnant.
Lynne Twist

Money is like manure. If you spread it around
it does a lot of good, but if you pile it up in one place
it stinks like hell.
Clint Murchison

Money is just a fertilizer. It can feed
nightmares or dreams.
Sharon Riddell

When starting out, don't worry about not having
enough money. Limited funds are a blessing,
not a curse. Nothing encourages creative thinking
in quite the same way.

H. Jackson Brown

I thank fate for having made me born poor. Poverty taught
me the true value of the gifts useful to life.

Anatole France

A poor person who is unhappy is in a better position than
a rich person who is unhappy. Because the poor person has hope.
He thinks money would help.

Jean Kerr

Put not your trust in money, but put your money in trust.

Oliver Wendell Holmes

A lot of people will urge you to put some money in a bank,
and in fact—within reason—this is very good advice. But don't go
overboard. Remember, what you are doing is giving your money
to someone else to hold on to, and I think that it is worth keeping
in mind that the businessmen who run banks are so worried about
holding on to things that they put little chains on all their pens.

Miss Piggy

I don't have a savings account
because I don't know my mother's maiden name.
Paula Poundstone

Never invest your money in anything
that eats or needs repairing.
Billy Rose

Invest in yourself, your family, your friends, your planet,
if you want a HIGH return.
Sharon Riddell

Invest in inflation. It's the only thing going up.
Will Rogers

The safest way to double your money is to fold it over
once and put it in your pocket.
Kin Hubbard

Money can't buy love—
but it certainly puts you in a wonderful
bargaining position.
Harrison Baker

Money can't buy friends,
but you can get a better class of enemy.
Spike Milligan

Money won't buy happiness, but it will pay the salaries
of a large research staff to study the problem.
Bill Vaughan

I see no point in money except to buy off anxiety.
I don't want to be rich. I want to be unanxious.
Sir John Betjeman

Money is good for bribing yourself through
the inconveniences of life.
Gottfried Reinhardt

The most popular labor-saving device is still money.
Phyllis George

If you want money, ask for money.
"I am enjoying the large sums of money that flow into my life,
quickly and effortlessly, this or something better for my highest good
and the highest good of all concerned."
John-Roger & Peter McWilliams

Why is there always so much month left
at the end of the money?
Anonymous

I couldn't be out of money. I still have checks.
Attributed to Gracie Allen

The most beautiful words in the English language are "Check Enclosed."
Dorothy Parker

It's good to have money and the things
that money can buy; but it's good, too, to
check up once in a while and make sure that
you haven't lost the things that money can't buy.
George Horace Lorimer

Certainly there are lots of things in life
that money won't buy, but it's very funny—
Have you ever tried to buy them without money?
Ogden Nash

I can't take it with me I know
But will it last until I go?
Martha F. Newmeyer

Yesterday is a canceled check;
tomorrow is a promissory note;
today is the only cash you have.
Spend it wisely.
Anonymous

pain & pleasure

pain *n* suffering or distress

plea•sure *n* feeling of being pleased or gratified

Never a lip is curved with pain
That can't be kissed into smiles again.
Bret Harte

The trick is not how much pain you feel—
but how much joy you feel.
Any idiot can feel pain.
Life is full of excuses to feel pain,
excuses not to live,
excuses, excuses, excuses.
Erica Jong

Simply put, you believe that things
or people make you unhappy,
but this is not accurate.
You make yourself unhappy.
Wayne Dyer

What marks the artist
is his power to shape the material of pain we all have.
Lionel Trilling

You will not grow if you sit
in a beautiful flower garden,
but you will grow if you are sick,
in pain, experience losses,
and if you do not put your head in the sand,
but take the pain and learn to accept it,
not as a curse or punishment
but as a gift to you
with a very, very specific purpose.
Elisabeth Kübler-Ross

Pain is important;
how we evade it, how we succumb to it,
how we deal with it, how we transcend it.
Audre Lorde

Those who have suffered understand suffering
and therefore extend their hand.
Patti Smith

I don't think of all the misery
but the beauty that still remains.
Anne Frank

We tire of those pleasures we take,
but never of those we give.
John Petit-Senn

Pleasure: An agreeable feeling
caused by getting the last laugh, having the last word,
or paying the last installment.
Evan Esar

Pleasure is the only thing to live for.
Nothing ages like happiness.
Oscar Wilde

Why not seize the pleasure at once?
How often is happiness destroyed by preparation,
foolish preparation!
Jane Austen

The great pleasure in life is
doing what people say you cannot do.
Walter Bagehot

You find yourself refreshed in the presence of
cheerful people. Why not make an honest effort
to confer that pleasure on others?
Half the battle is gained if you never allow
yourself to say anything gloomy.
Lydia M. Child

One of the most lasting pleasures you can experience
is the feeling that comes over you when you genuinely
forgive an enemy—whether he knows it or not.
O. A. Battista

Think big thoughts but relish small pleasures.
H. Jackson Brown Jr.

s

stress & burnout
success & failure

stress *n* an upsetting condition caused by adverse external influences

burn•out *n* physical or emotional exhaustion

The chief cause of stress is reality.
Lily Tomlin

No one can escape stress, but you can learn
to cope with it. Practice positive thinking...
seize control in small ways.
Adele Scheele

I read this article. It said the typical symptoms
of stress are eating too much, smoking too much,
impulse buying and driving too fast.
Are they kidding? This is my idea of a great day!
Monica Piper

Stress is the resistance to what's happening right now.
As we allow ourselves to open to this moment fully,
there is absolutely no stress.
Stephan Rechtschaffen

Stress is basically a disconnection from the earth,
a forgetting of the breath. Stress is an ignorant state.
It believes that everything is an emergency.
Nothing is that important. Just lie down.
Natalie Goldberg

Keep breathing.
Sophie Tucker

Stress—that confusion created when the mind must
override the body's basic desire to choke the living #*?!@
out of some idiot who desperately needs it.
Office sign

Nothing is more destined to create deep-seated anxieties
in people than the false assumption that
life should be free from anxieties.
Archbishop Fulton J. Sheen

If I knew what I was so anxious about,
I wouldn't be so anxious.
Mignon McLaughlin

Nothing erases unpleasant thoughts more effectively
than conscious concentration on pleasant ones.
Hans Selye

If you can't help it, don't think about it.
Carmel Myers

For fast acting relief, try slowing down.
Lily Tomlin

suc•cess *n* the achievement of something desired

fail•ure *n* not achieving the desired end

Success is never a destination—it's a journey.
Satenig St. Marie

Success is that old A B C—ability, breaks, and courage.
Charles Luckman

Success is simply a matter of luck. Ask any failure.
Earl Wilson

Success is often achieved by those
who don't know that failure is inevitable.
Coco Chanel

Success to me is having ten honeydew melons
and eating only the top half of each one.
Barbra Streisand

Success has gone to my hips.
Dolly Parton

Life is a series of moments,
to live each one is to succeed.
Corita Kent

There is only one success—
to be able to spend your life in your own way.
Christopher Morley

Success has nothing to do with what you gain in life or
accomplish for yourself. It's what you do for others.
Danny Thomas

I must admit that I personally measure success
in terms of the contributions an individual makes
to her or his fellow human beings.
Margaret Mead

A true measure of your worth includes
all the benefits others have gained from your success.
Cullen Hightower

Success isn't measured by the position you reach in life;
it's measured by the obstacles you overcome.
Booker T. Washington

I owe my success to having listened respectfully
to the very best advice, and then going away
and doing the exact opposite.
G. K. Chesterton

If I wanted to become a tramp, I would seek information
and advice from the most successful tramp I could find.
If I wanted to become a failure, I would seek advice from
men who have never succeeded. If I wanted to succeed in
all things, I would look around me for those who are
succeeding, and do as they have done.

Joseph Marshall Wade

Decide what you want, decide what you are willing to
exchange for it. Establish your priorities and go to work.

H. L. Hunt

Be like a postage stamp—
stick to one thing till you get there.

Josh Billings

You can have anything you want if you want it
desperately enough. You must want it with an inner
exuberance that erupts through the skin and joins
the energy that created the world.

Sheila Graham

To be successful, the first thing to do is
fall in love with your work.

Sister Mary Lauretta

If you don't do it excellently, don't do it at all.
Because if it's not excellent, it won't be profitable or fun,
and if you're not in business for fun or profit,
what the hell are you doing there?
Robert Townsend

What I wanted was to be allowed to do the thing
in the world that I did best—which I believed then
and believe now is the greatest privilege there is.
When I did that success found me.
Debbi Fields

Make no little plans; they have no magic to stir men's
blood....Make big plans, aim high in hope and work.
Daniel H. Burnham

Don't be afraid to take a big step if one is indicated.
You can't cross a chasm in two small jumps.
David Lloyd George

You can have big plans,
but it's the small choices that have the greatest power.
They draw us toward the future we want to create.
Robert Cooper

Far better it is to dare mighty things,
to win glorious triumphs even though
checkered by failures, than to rank with those
poor spirits who neither enjoy nor suffer much
because they live in the gray twilight
that knows neither victory nor defeat.

Theodore Roosevelt

Victory is won not in miles but in inches. Win a little now,
hold your ground, and later, win a little more.

Louis L'Amour

Shoot for the moon.
Even if you miss it you will land among the stars.

Les Brown

Some succeed because they are destined to;
most succeed because they are determined to.

Anatole France

When I thought I couldn't go on, I forced myself to keep
going. My success is based on persistence, not luck.

Estee Lauder

Nothing in the world can take the place of persistence.
Talent will not; Genius will not; Education will not;
Persistence and determination alone are omnipotent.

Calvin Coolidge

On the secret to success: Early to bed, early to rise,
work like hell, and advertise.

Gertrude Boyle

The only place you find success before work
is in the dictionary.

May V. Smith

If at first you don't succeed
you're running about average.

M. H. Alderson

Success is getting what you want;
happiness is wanting what you get.

Anonymous

That man is a success who has lived well,
laughed often and loved much.

Robert Louis Stevenson

Let no feeling of discouragement prey upon you,
and in the end you are sure to succeed.

Abraham Lincoln

There is but one secret to success—never give up!

Ben Nighthorse Campbell

To laugh often and much, to win the respect
of intelligent people and the affection of children;
to earn the appreciation of honest critics and endure
the betrayal of false friends; to appreciate beauty;
to find the best in others; to leave the world a bit better,
whether by a healthy child, a garden patch
or a redeemed social condition; to know even one life has
breathed easier because you have lived.
This is to have succeeded.

Ralph Waldo Emerson

Success is a state of mind.
If you want success, start thinking of yourself as a success.

Joyce Brothers

If you have made mistakes...there is always another
chance for you...you may have a fresh start any moment
you choose, for this thing we call "failure" is not
the falling down, but the staying down.

Mary Pickford

Only those who dare to fail greatly
can ever achieve greatly.

Robert Kennedy

Our greatest glory is not in never failing,
but in rising up every time we fail.
Ralph Waldo Emerson

Fall seven times, stand up eight.
Japanese saying

For every failure, there's an alternative
course of action. You just have to find it.
When you come to a roadblock, take a detour.
Mary Kay Ash

Failure is the opportunity
to begin again more intelligently.
Henry Ford

There is much to be said for failure.
It is more interesting than success.
Max Beerbohm

To lose
Is to learn.
Anonymous

Failure is success if we learn from it.
Malcolm Forbes

Don't think of it as failure.
Think of it as time-released success.
Robert Orben

There is no failure except in no longer trying.
Elbert Hubbard

You may be disappointed if you fail,
but you are doomed if you don't try.
Beverly Sills

Never let the fear of striking out get in your way.
Babe Ruth

Do not be afraid of defeat. You are never so near to
victory as when defeated in a good cause.
Henry Ward Beecher

Remember that a kick in the ass is a step forward.
Anonymous

Act as though it were impossible to fail.
Dorothea Brande

Keep your eye on your heroes, not on your zeroes.
Robert H. Schuller

I don't know the key to success,
but the key to failure is trying to please everybody.
Bill Cosby

Quit now, you'll never make it.
If you disregard this advice, you'll be halfway there.
David Zucker

If at first you don't succeed,
do it the way your wife told you to.
Yvonne Knepper

To those who need encouragement, remember this:
Beware of quitting too soon. Dr. Seuss' first children's
book was rejected by 23 publishers.
The 24th publisher sold 6 million copies.
Ann Landers

time & technology
travel troubles

time *n*   an interval separating two points of a continuum

tech•nol•o•gy *n*   the scientific method used to achieve an
   objective

Nothing is ours except time.
Seneca

Counting time is not so important as making time count.
James J. Walker

Time:
Nature's way of preventing everything
from happening at once.
Evan Esar

You lose a lot of time hating people.
Marian Anderson

One always has time enough, if one will apply it well.
Johann Wolfgang von Goethe

The time you enjoy wasting is not wasted time.
Bertrand Russell

Nothing puzzles me more than time and space;
and yet nothing troubles me less,
as I never think about them.
Charles Lamb

I never think of the future. It comes soon enough.
Albert Einstein

Time wounds all heels.
Bennett Cerf

I would I could stand on a busy corner, hat in hand, and
beg people to throw me all their wasted hours.
Bernard Berenson

If it weren't for Philo T. Farnsworth, inventor of television,
we'd still be eating frozen radio dinners.
Johnny Carson

If it weren't for electricity
we'd all be watching television by candlelight.
George Gobel

Computers are useless. They can only give you answers.
Pablo Picasso

Television enables you to be entertained in your home
by people you wouldn't have in your home.
David Frost

Thanks to television, for the first time the young are seeing
history made before it is censored by their elders.
Margaret Mead

I find television very educational. Every time someone turns
on the set I go into the other room and read a book.
Groucho Marx

Television has proved that people will look at anything
rather than each other.
Ann Landers

There is no reason anyone would want
a computer in their home.
Ken Olson, founder of Digital Equipment Corp., 1977

I think there is a world market for maybe five computers.
Thomas Watson, Chairman of IBM, 1943

Computers in the future may weigh
no more than 1.5 tons.
Popular Mechanics, 1949

Computers make it easy to do a lot of things,
but most of the things they make it easier to do,
don't need to be done.
Andy Rooney

To err is human, but to really foul things up
requires a computer.
Anonymous

This telephone has too many shortcomings
to be seriously considered as a means of communication.
The device is inherently of no value to us.
Western Union internal memo, 1876

Fax machine:
A device that allows someone in another state
to pile work on your desk.
Mrs. Webster's Guide to Business

One machine can do the work of fifty ordinary men.
No machine can do the work of one extraordinary man.
Elbert Hubbard

trav•el *v*   to go from one place to another

The journey, not the arrival, matters;
the voyage, not the landing.
Paul Theroux

It is good to have an end to journey towards;
but it is the journey that matters, in the end.
Ursula K. LeGuin

To travel hopefully is a better thing than to arrive.
Robert Louis Stevenson

Ride the horse in the direction that it's going.
Werner Erhard

It isn't how much time you spend somewhere that makes it
memorable; it's how you spend the time.
David Brenner

The really happy man
is one who can enjoy the scenery on a detour.
Anonymous

Humor is the traveler's first line of defense.
Travel without humor is like sex without love.
You can do it, but what's the point really?
Mary Morris

The scientific theory I like best is that the rings of Saturn
are composed entirely of lost airline luggage.
Mark Russell

He who would travel happily must travel light.
Antoine de Saint-Exupéry

I never travel without my diary.
One should always have something sensational to read.
Oscar Wilde

It is easier to find a traveling companion
than to get rid of one.
Art Buchwald

Never play peek-a-boo with a child on a long plane trip.
There's no end to the game.
Finally I grabbed him by the bib and said,
"Look, it's always gonna be me!"
Rita Rudner

A wise man travels to discover himself.
James Russell Lowell

Though we travel the world over to find the beautiful,
we must carry it with us or we find it not.
Ralph Waldo Emerson

Keep things on your trip in perspective, and you'll be
amazed at the perspective you'll gain on things back
home while you're away....One's little world is put into
perspective by the bigger world out there.
Gail Rubin Bereny

A man travels the world over in search of what he needs
and returns home to find it.
George Moore

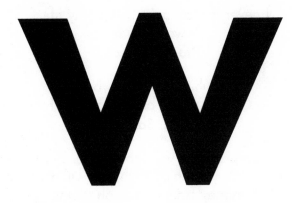

**work weary
worrywarts**

work *n* effort directed toward the accomplishment of something

---

I never did a day's work in my life.
It was all fun.
Thomas Edison

Nothing is really work
unless you would rather be doing something else.
J. M. Barrie

In the long run you will receive more from life
doing the job you enjoy than you will ever earn
in money from a job you loathe.
Terry L. Mayfield

Do What You Love, the Money Will Follow
Marsha Sinetar

The secret of joy in work
is contained in one word—excellence.
To know how to do something well is to enjoy it.
Pearl S. Buck

The supreme accomplishment is
to blur the line between work and play.
Arthur Toynbee

It is amazing how much people can get done
if they do not worry about who gets the credit.
Sandra Swinney

Anyone can do any amount of work,
provided it isn't the work
he is supposed to be doing at that moment.
Robert Benchley

I long to accomplish a great and noble task,
but it is my chief duty to accomplish small tasks
as if they were great and noble.
Helen Keller

All labor that uplifts humanity has dignity and importance
and should be undertaken with painstaking excellence.
Martin Luther King, Jr.

Every morning I get up and look through
the Forbes list of the richest people in America.
If I'm not there, I go to work.
Robert Orben

I don't have anything against work.
I just figure, why deprive somebody who really loves it?
Dobie Gillis

Work is what you do so that some time
you won't have to do it anymore.
Alfred Polgar

Hard work never killed anybody,
but why take a chance?
Charlie McCarthy (Edgar Bergen)

If you have a job without aggravations,
you don't have a job.
Malcolm Forbes

The highest reward for a man's toil
is not what he gets for it
but what he becomes by it.
John Ruskin

What makes you worthwhile is who you are,
not what you do.
Marianne Williams

Generate so much loving energy that people want
to just come and hang out with you.
And when they show up, bill them!
Stuart Wilde

Occasionally indulging in a do-nothing day
is more than worth the price.
Malcolm Forbes

wor•ry *v* to feel concerned or uneasy about something

Don't worry. Be happy.
Meher Baba

Worry a little every day
and in a lifetime you will lose a couple of years.
If something is wrong, fix it if you can.
But train yourself not to worry.
Worry never fixes anything.
Mary Hemingway

There is no good in arguing with the inevitable.
The only argument with an east wind
is to put on your overcoat.
James Russell Lowell

Worry does not empty tomorrow of its sorrow,
it empties today of its joy.
Anonymous

Don't waste the years struggling for things
that are unimportant. Don't destroy your peace of mind
by looking back, worrying about the past.
Live in the present, enjoy the present.
Henry David Thoreau

You're only here for a short visit.
Don't hurry, don't worry.
And be sure to smell the flowers along the way.
Walter Hagen

If you keep on saying things are going to be bad,
you have a good chance of being a prophet.
Isaac Bashevis Singer

Money is another pressure.
I'm not complaining,
I'm just saying that there's a certain luxury
in having no money. I spent ten years in New York
not having it, not worrying about it.
Suddenly you have it, then you worry,
where is it going?
Am I doing the right thing with it?
Dustin Hoffman

You cannot prevent the birds of sorrow
from flying over your head,
but you can prevent them
from building nests in your hair.

Chinese saying

Walk away from it until you're stronger.
All your problems will be there when you get back,
but you'll be better able to cope.

Lady Bird Johnson

When I look back on all the worries
I remember the story of the old man
who said on his deathbed
that he had had a lot of trouble in his life,
most of which never happened.

Winston Churchill

What we anticipate seldom occurs;
what we least expected generally happens.

Benjamin Disraeli

Worry often gives a small thing a big shadow.

Swedish saying

Worry is interest paid on trouble before it falls due.

Dean Inge

The game is supposed to be fun.
If you have a bad day, don't worry about it.
You can't expect to get a hit every game.
Yogi Berra

Most of my major disappointments
have turned out to be blessings in disguise.
So whenever anything bad does happen to me,
I kind of sit back and feel, well,
if I give this enough time,
it'll turn out that this was good,
so I shan't worry about it too much.
William Gaines

Even in the deepest sinking there is the hidden purpose of
an ultimate rising. Thus it is for all men, from none is the
source of light withheld unless he himself withdraws from it.
Therefore the most important thing is not to despair.
Hasidic saying

My advice to actresses is don't worry about your looks.
The very thing that makes you unhappy in your
apprearance may be the one thing to make you a star.
Estelle Winwood

You'll have a better day if you think about where you're going than what's stuck to the bottom of your shoes.
Tammy Hansen Gilbert

There are two days about which nobody should ever worry, and these are yesterday and tomorrow.
Robert J. Burdette

What me worry?
Alfred E. Neuman

INDEX TO AUTHORS

Benchley, Robert 147
benShea, Noah 51
Berenson, Bernard 139
Bereny, Gail Rubin 144
Berle, Milton 43
Bernhardt, Sarah 96
Berra, Yogi 153
Betjeman, Sir John 115
Bettelheim, Bruno 76
Beudoin, Patricia C. 70
Bierce, Ambrose 11
Billings, Josh 64, 129
Bloomfield, Harold H. 67
Boeme, Ludwig 97
Boetcker, W. J. 110
Bohn, H. G. 53
Bombeck, Erma 43, 46, 67, 69, 71, 81
Bonnell, John Sutherland 90
Boosler, Elayne 31, 105
Bottome, Phyllis 11
Boyle, Gertrude 132
Bradstreet, Anne 15
Brande, Dorothea 135
Bray, Ann Eliza 78
Brenner, David 142
Brooks, Mel 96
Brothers, Joyce 28, 133
Brown, H. Jackson 80, 96, 113, 121
Brown, Hobart 110
Brown, Les 131
Brown, Rita Mae 95
Browne, Merry 111
Bucella, Marty 5
Buchman, Frank 112
Buchwald, Art 143

Buck, Glen 65
Buck, Pearl S. 37, 146
Buddha 62, 99
Buechner, Frederick 36
Bumper sticker 82
Burdette, Robert J. 154
Burke, Billie 4
Burnett, Carol 22
Burnham, Daniel H. 130
Burns, George 5, 7, 39, 58
Burton, Richard 56
Buscaglia, Leo 92
Bush, Barbara 69
Butler, Samuel 37, 92
Byrne, Robert 31, 94
Campbell, Ben Nighthorse 132
Campbell, Thomas 36
Carlyle, Thomas 65
Carnegie, Dale 64
Carson, Johnny 37, 139
Carson, Rachel 79
Carter, Judy 107
Cerf, Bennett 139
Chanel, Coco 127
Charles, C. Leslie 38
Cher 27, 107
Chesterton, G. K. 128
Chevalier, Maurice 3
Child, Lydia M. 120
Chinese saying 11, 23, 152
Ching, Cyrus 13
Christie, Agatha 29
Churchill, Winston 39, 94, 152
Cicero 36
Clark, Karen Kaiser 20

ABOUT THE AUTHOR

Allen Klein, also known as "Mr. Jollytologist," is an award-winning professional speaker and best-selling author. He travels worldwide showing audiences how to deal with not-so-funny stuff. In addition to this book, Klein is also the author of four other books—

- *Quotations to Cheer You Up When the World is Getting You Down*
- *Wing Tips*
- *The Courage to Laugh*
- *The Healing Power of Humor*

For more information about Klein or his presentations, contact him either on the web at www.allenklein.com or by mail at 1034 Page Street, San Francisco, CA 94117.